IMAGES
of America

# THE WHITE CHURCH
# OF BLANDFORD

IMAGES
*of America*

# THE WHITE CHURCH
# OF BLANDFORD

Nicholas J. Aieta
Foreword by Pliny Norcross III

ARCADIA
PUBLISHING

Copyright © 2022 by Nicholas J. Aieta
ISBN 978-1-4671-0794-5

Published by Arcadia Publishing
Charleston, South Carolina

Printed in the United States of America

Library of Congress Control Number: 2021947206

For all general information, please contact Arcadia Publishing:
Telephone 843-853-2070
Fax 843-853-0044
E-mail sales@arcadiapublishing.com
For customer service and orders:
Toll-Free 1-888-313-2665

Visit us on the Internet at www.arcadiapublishing.com

*Dedicated to the many people who have contributed to collecting the history of the White Church and its restoration and ongoing preservation.*

# CONTENTS

# FOREWORD

With the 200th anniversary approaching of the White Church of Blandford's 1822 construction, the Blandford Historical Society, current owner of this iconic structure, decided that the building's fascinating history should be thoroughly chronicled in the form of a published book. In addition to a brief examination of the individual lives of those who set the stage for the building's eventual construction and stewardship, this book describes numerous challenges presented by periodic major restorations and also gives a picture of the structure's current and future use. Originally designed by one of the region's preeminent 19th-century architects, Isaac Damon, the 200th-anniversary celebration of Blandford's National Register of Historic Places church will culminate with the completion of a major 18-month restoration project in the summer of 2023.

Key to the preservation of the building has been the steady hand and leadership from Peter Hamm of Historic Preservation Associates. Starting in the early 1990s, Peter has worked on multiple levels of the restoration process for the White Church. Dedicated to the preservation of architecture in New England, Peter's leadership has been essential in keeping the church square with its architectural roots, originated by Isaac Damon in 1822.

In searching for someone who would be able and willing to accept the substantial task of authoring this book, the society was delighted that Prof. Nicholas Aieta, PhD, chair of the Westfield State University History Department and a specialist in early American history, enthusiastically accepted this substantial writing challenge. Professor Aieta's familiarity with Arcadia Publishing's process was an enormous help in structuring this project.

The Blandford Historical Society is deeply appreciative of the tremendous financial support given to this entire restoration mission, from numerous individual donors and fundraising events to very generous grant awards by the Massachusetts Cultural Council and surrounding local arts councils. We hope this book gives the reader an increased understanding of why the White Church of Blandford is considered a regional historic treasure.

—Pliny Norcross III

# ACKNOWLEDGMENTS

Thanks and acknowledgements to the many contributors of the Blandford Historical Society past, present, and future who have preserved these documents and made the story, text, and image reproduction possible.

My research assistant Michael E. Ibscher chased down a number of leads related to Isaac Damon's design career while also identifying possible image candidates for inclusion in the text.

The staff at Arcadia Publishing who assisted me on this project and helped bring it to a successful conclusion were Caroline (Anderson) Vickerson and Jeff Ruetsche. Jeff's initial enthusiasm, guidance, and support were greatly appreciated. In particular, Caroline's patience and direction as we worked through various drafts of the text were extremely helpful and essential.

My partner, Heather Wyman, made numerous suggestions to the text and pushed questions which I had not considered, thereby improving the final version.

Finally, special thanks to my children, Willa and Callum, who did not get much time from their father during the push to complete this book, for their spirit in taking part in a variety of historical and fundraising events connected to its completion.

Unless otherwise noted, all images are courtesy of the Blandford Historical Society.

# INTRODUCTION

Two hundred years ago, in mid-June 1822, the cornerstone for a new meetinghouse was laid in Blandford, Massachusetts. The principal architect was Isaac Damon of nearby Northampton, Massachusetts. The meetinghouse was to be the home to the Congregational community of Blandford, though in the ensuing 200 years, it became much more. The White Church, as it is currently known, remains a symbol on the town seal, a historic landmark, and a center for town activity, even if it no longer houses an active congregation. The White Church was neither the first church constructed in the community nor the only house of worship to be embraced by the mixed Scots-Irish and English colonists who moved into the region in the 18th century.

Originally, the lands on which the church sits had been utilized and seasonally inhabited by members of the Algonquin-speaking people of the region who were part of the Pocumtuck Confederacy. In 1732, the land was surveyed and later divided into lots by English colonial administrators. Between 1732 and 1735, petitions to the General Court in Boston resulted in the surveying and establishment of numerous town plots between Westfield (incorporated by the General Court in 1669) and Sheffield, some 40 miles to the west. These communities and the roads that connected them developed partially on lands gifted to the Massachusetts government by the Stockbridge Mohicans, who had established their own town in 1734.

The newest towns included Sheffield itself (1733) and New Glasgow (1735), the latter of which was renamed Blandford in 1741 when the community applied for incorporation. The name Blandford was chosen by the provincial governor, William Shirley, who had arrived from England on a ship of the same name in 1731.

The earliest residents of Blandford arrived from Hopkinton, Massachusetts, dissatisfied with the church organization in that community. This fact meant that the meetinghouse in Blandford was originally organized under Presbyterian auspices, the transition to New England Congregational worship coming over 60 years later. By 1765, the population had grown to 406 residents divided among 68 households.

Blandford was and remains a rural community with land dedicated to agricultural pursuits. In the earliest days, with limited arable land, community members leaned on dairy production and livestock raising. Timber harvesting was likely, and as with many such communities, subsistence farming was a key component of the town's development. By 1776, Blandford residents had built mills and a tannery, and the town had grown to 772 inhabitants. The town's population continued to expand in the aftermath of American independence, reaching its highest point in history of 1,778 persons in 1800, about the same time the transition to Congregational worship occurred.

After the White Church was constructed, it remained the primary seat of the Congregational community until another house of worship was constructed close by but off the hill. During the first seven decades of the 20th century, church members used the "town" church in the colder months of the year, returning to the hill in the summer.

Although the basic structure of the White Church remained the same, modifications, renovations, and adjustments have been made over the two centuries both to suit the needs of the congregation and to preserve the structure. Within 45 years of construction, the church's axis was shifted to accommodate the needs of a new addition to the congregation—music in the form of an organ. Just under half a century later, as a new organ was installed, the building went through further alterations.

Eventually, as the building surpassed 150 years in age, time began to catch up with the structure, and a variety of challenges faced the congregation and the structure in the last 20 years of the 20th century. With a need for massive repairs, the community and the congregation came together to begin the process of saving the building.

In 1992, the White Church Restoration Committee was formed, and a goal of raising $250,000 was established. At the very least, the restoration was to include a mixture of paint removal and repainting, wire brushing and painting the roof, repairing the foundation, and installing a new porch on the south side of the building. Additional goals were established to redo electric and water service, build a new septic system, and repair windows and the plaster as well as the tin ceiling on the inside.

By the fall of 1993, the White Church Restoration Committee, cochaired by Sumner Robbins and Ann Southworth, with members Chuck Benson, Anita Forish, Nancy Lewis, Ed Lewis, Bob Murphy, and Sally Robbins, had spearheaded efforts that reached over one-third of this goal. During the Blandford Fair, volunteers connected to the committee worked to park cars, and a myriad of other fundraising efforts were implemented that helped raise awareness of the restoration efforts as well as the necessary funds.

For example, a Back to Blandford Weekend, hosted on July 24 and 25, 1993, invited former Blandford residents back to the community. The effort netted over 110 former residents and their families who went on cemetery tours, experienced a church service in the White Church, and raised funds through an auction hosted at the elementary school. By the end of Back to Blandford Weekend, the group had raised nearly $8,000.

Events such as these highlighted the town of Blandford while also reminding people that the historic landmark was worthy of restoration. In the early 1990s, the committee emphasized that the White Church was to be open for a variety of community events, regardless of affiliation with the congregation. The White Church therefore was to be available for weddings, baptisms, funerals, church services, concerts, award ceremonies, and more. The restoration committee noted that key early fundraising came from the National Trust for Historic Preservation and a matching grant from the Frank Stanley Beveridge Foundation.

As Thanksgiving approached in 1993, the White Church Restoration Committee celebrated its successes, thanked donors who came from both the local community and across the United States, and launched an ambitious plan for the coming year. On the final Saturday of July 1994, the committee planned a Scottish festival. The festival was intended to both connect with the history of Blandford and serve as a new annual fundraiser for the White Church. By the time the Blandford Historical Society purchased it in 2006, these years of effort cemented the legacy of the White Church in Blandford.

# One

# BLANDFORD AND THE FIRST CONGREGATION IS BORN

## 1735–1805

Meetinghouses held important positions in New England towns, and Blandford, Massachusetts, was no exception. These spaces were intended as both religious and civil authority meeting halls. When the Scots-Irish settlers arrived in Blandford, they were leaving their homes in Hopkinton, Massachusetts, because of a religious disagreement. Residents in Hopkinton had voted in a Congregational method of worship, and these Scots-Irish preferred a Presbyterian form.

In 1734, these families had organized their own Presbyterian church in Hopkinton with the aid of Rev. Thomas Prince (1687–1758) of Boston. As land on the Massachusetts–Connecticut border had been organized by the General Court of the Province of Massachusetts, these Hopkinton Presbyterians made the move west in 1735, establishing themselves in what they endeavored to call Glasgow Lands. Eventually, the town was named Blandford in honor of the ship that bore the provincial governor to the New World.

Rev. John Keep's early history of the town and church in Blandford revealed that while a meetinghouse was not constructed immediately, a rude structure, frame only, was built in 1740. The frame was not covered until 1741, and glass windows for the meetinghouse were not installed until 1753. The early meetinghouse also had no flooring until that same year.

The first minister in Blandford, William McClenathan (or McClanachan), was installed in 1744. A native of Ireland and educated at Edinburgh, he came to New England in 1734 working first in what is now Maine (Georgetown and Portland) before arriving in Blandford. Serving as a chaplain in the British army starting in 1745, McClenathan became unpopular when a number of Blandford residents were lost during the Louisbourg campaign in Canada, and though he served in both the Chelsea and Revere areas of Massachusetts, Blandford's community did not welcome him back.

James Morton, also a native of Ireland and born the same year (1714) as McClenathan, was settled as minister in 1747, beginning a stormy 20-year service as Blandford's spiritual leader. Morton's "liberal" interpretation of alcohol production and consumption did not sit well with Blandford residents, though he remained a resident of the community after his dismissal in 1767 and until his death in 1793.

For 20 years following, Blandford did not have regular religious leadership until Revolutionary War veteran and Yale graduate Joseph Badger was installed in 1787. For example, Joseph Patrick was installed at Blandford in June 1772, but the congregation dismissed him in December!

This monument was placed in July 1903. Its purpose was to denote that "Ye old first church of the frontier town of Blandford Mass. stood on this spot. Begun 1740 Finished 1805."

The marker includes the additional words *Vox Clamantis in Deserto*. This Latin phrase is usually translated as "a voice crying in the wilderness" and is also the motto of Dartmouth College.

The history of the congregation was long preserved, including this pulpit chair used by Rev. William McClenathan (1744–1746). The chair may have been preserved by Rev. John Keep (1805–1821), the last minister to preach in the old meetinghouse. As Keep lived in a home owned by Enos W. Boise, the chair fell into the possession of the Boise family, and by 1984, the chair was back in use at the pulpit of the White Church.

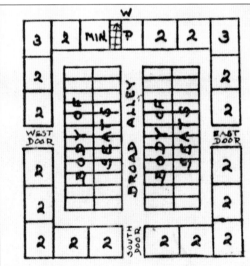

Plan of Meeting House 1760

W = Window
P = = Pulpit
Min. = Ministerial Pew
Numbers-Designate families seated in each pew.

This plan of the original meetinghouse, c. 1760, was drawn from descriptions provided by Rev. John Keep and church records. Town historian Doris W. Hayden reproduced this plan for the 1976 bicentennial year from work originally done by former minister Sumner Gilbert Wood (1901–1911).

The following quotation shows the words inscribed on one of Rev. James Morton's (1747–1767) gravestones: "Memento Mori / In Memory of the late Rev James Morton who was born in Middletown in the County of Armagh & Kingdom of Ireland in 1714 and died Oct 1 1793. Here lies the Husband Parent faithful friend, The once loved Pastor's labours here doth end. May you who once the Pastor's warnings heard Now contemplate the day and stand prepar'd To meet your doom, your last & just reward." (Courtesy of Pliny Norcross III.)

James Morton's cemetery stone features a tree, which was a symbol used often around the end of the 18th century and in the early 19th century to memorialize life. As the tree appears full and with sprouting leaves, it was likely intended to indicate life everlasting, an appropriate message for the former minister.

This c. 1799 plan of the original meetinghouse, also reproduced by Doris W. Hayden, turns the meetinghouse on its axis, recalling the church's proximity to North Street and indicating access to gallery stairs and a porch not noted in the 1760 rendition.

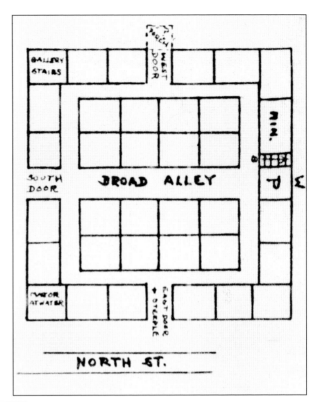

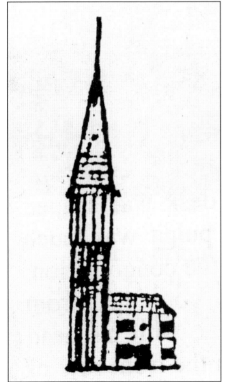

An imagined rendering shows the exterior of the first meetinghouse as it may have appeared once subscribers had raised enough funds to construct the steeple. This meetinghouse stood on the western side of North Street, opposite the present location of the White Church. Rev. John Keep served as pastor in the last year of this meetinghouse's use.

15

Rev. Joseph Badger served as minister in Blandford from 1787 until 1800, shortly after completing his studies at Yale in New Haven, Connecticut. Badger was recruited by the Connecticut Missionary Society in 1800 to serve in what was then the Connecticut Western Reserve (modern-day Ohio).

This is the memorial stone for Sarah Badger, daughter of Lois and Rev. Joseph Badger. She died October 27, 1795, aged three years, seven months, while Reverend Badger was doing work in what would become Ohio. The stone reads: "The little Child was dear to me But just and right was that decree Which brought her to Eternity." (Courtesy of Pliny Norcross III.)

# Two

# THE WHITE CHURCH AND ISAAC DAMON

## 1805–1822

By February 1821, several generations of Blandford's Christians had worshipped in three different churches. Most met at the oldest established church, where a split occurred in 1799 when a Protestant Episcopal Society was formed. In the early winter of 1821, the first religious society of Blandford voted to create a three-person committee and inform the Episcopal Society of the intent to build a new meetinghouse. Further, the committee sought to heal the divide, asking whether the Protestant Episcopal Society was willing to join in constructing the new house.

In the late autumn and early winter of 1821, having determined to proceed with construction, a committee was chosen to agree upon a location for the church. Two different regions of the town were represented in this selection. The committee agreed to include three disinterested parties from outside of Blandford to serve as mediators for selecting a location.

On December 19, 1821, the committee reported the chosen location. Sylvester Emmons, Ashael Wright, and Nered Elder noted that the decision making had been harmonious and demonstrated a respectable positivity within Blandford. The committee agreed that it would be best to build the worship house on town-owned land close to where the current first society meetinghouse stood. The committee was satisfied that the town's residents would be best served by such a location.

The location on North Road being chosen, a new committee consisting of Abner Gibbs, Eli Holt, Abenson Knox, Samuel Knox, and Orrin Sage was developed to oversee the construction. This committee contracted with Isaac Damon of Northampton on February 11, 1822, to build the new house of worship. The cost was to be $4,600. Damon began his work in the spring of 1822, completing the project by mid-October.

Isaac Damon, born in Weymouth, Massachusetts, in 1782, was about 40 years old when he was contracted to build the White Church. Damon had worked as a carpenter and studied architecture, moving to Northampton by 1811. His first project in the region was a church construction in Northampton, and by the 1820s, Damon had his hand in everything from courthouses and jails to factories, warehouses, bridges, and churches. Damon was described as a man of great energy and physical vigor, generous, and a leader in public affairs. These attributes, along with his experience erecting churches in Westhampton and Springfield, may have come to the attention of Blandford residents, inspiring them to work with Damon.

Rev. John Keep served as minister from 1805 until just before the White Church's construction in 1822, leaving the area in May 1821; he had agreed to serve as minister only because the members committed to shifting from Presbyterianism to the Congregational form of worship. In March of that year, Keep offered a discourse on the history of the First Congregational Church, noting that he had to work hard to re-create the history as early records were sparse. Initially drawn to Homer, New York, Keep eventually moved on to Ohio and became one of the early trustees at what became Oberlin College. A committed abolitionist, Keep also cast the deciding vote allowing African American students to attend Oberlin.

Architect Isaac Damon and his second wife, Sophia Strong Damon, were captured in this daguerreotype by Jeremiah D. Wells of Northampton, Massachusetts. Damon had come to Northampton in relation to the construction of the First Congregational Church of Northampton in 1811–1812 and wed Sophia in 1813. (Courtesy of Historic Northampton.)

The Westhampton, Massachusetts, Congregational Church was designed and built by Isaac Damon in 1816–1817. The church is striking in its similarity to Blandford's White Church, mirroring its five-over-five window and door design on the front. (Courtesy of Historic Northampton.)

Isaac Damon undoubtedly was aided in his architectural pursuits through consulting Benjamin Ashers's *The Country Builder's Assistant: The Rudiments of Architecture, the American Builder's Companion, The Practical House Carpenter and Practice of Architecture.* Perhaps Damon made use of the 1805 edition, published in Greenfield, Massachusetts. This side elevation may have served as an inspiration for Damon's design of the White Church. (Courtesy of Library of Congress.)

The First Church in Springfield, Massachusetts, organized a century prior to Blandford's founding, hired Isaac Damon several years before Blandford to design its new home. While there are some similarities, notable differences, such as the lack of columns in Blandford, exist as well. (Courtesy of Library of Congress.)

In addition to churches, Isaac Damon worked on bridge design in New England and New York. The Tucker Toll Bridge, connecting Bellows Falls, Vermont, to North Walpole, New Hampshire, was built in 1840 and was replaced in 1930. (Courtesy of Library of Congress.)

The Old Toll Bridge, crossing the Connecticut River at Springfield, Massachusetts, was constructed in 1816, the builder being Isaac Damon. While partially damaged in 1818 and again in 1820, the bridge was repaired and remained in use until the 1920s, when it was replaced by Memorial Bridge. (Courtesy of Library of Congress.)

The Southwick Congregational Church (Massachusetts) was built in 1823–1824 by Isaac Damon shortly after the White Church in Blandford. The building is very closely related in design to the Springfield First Church with four columns in front and an almost identical belfry. (Courtesy of Nicholas J. Aieta.)

A very different type of construction was used by Isaac Damon some eight years later when he built the Congregational church in what is now East Granby, Connecticut. Instead of building primarily with wood, Damon made use of ashlar granite when designing and building this church. (Courtesy of Library of Congress.)

# *Three*

# CHANGE COMES TO THE WHITE CHURCH
## 1830s–1900

The first minister to serve in the newly constructed church was Dorus Clarke (1823–1835). Reverend Clarke and his successor, Charles J. Hinsdale (1835–1863), oversaw one of the more consistent leadership periods in the White Church's history, as the two men combined to minister the flock for nearly 40 years.

Originally, when congregants entered the church, they might head to the stairs leading to the galleries above or into the main seating area of pews. As worshippers entered, they would pass immediately by the pulpit, which was placed in a tall semicircular niche underneath the church tower. This raised pulpit put the minister in position well above even those who were standing on the church floor. Near the east aisle, the minister could climb a set of interior stairs into the pulpit. The height was such that it placed the minister close to the same level as those who sat in the front row of pews in the gallery.

During Reverend Hinsdale's tenure, the congregation agreed to allow musical instruments to become part of the service. In addition to a choir that at one point peaked at 80 voices, the church had a violin, harmonium melodeon, flute, bass, and double bass.

Following the American Civil War, major renovations began, and the raised pulpit was removed and the pews reversed. The minister now led from the north end of the building, and to the south, a large Johnson pipe organ was placed in the alcove, with pews for the choir just above. This shift necessitated several additional changes. From 1822 to 1866, the north wall had three sets of windows matching those to the east and west. These windows were removed and sets of platforms were constructed to house the new pulpit. Originally, there were side aisles and pews colloquially referred to as "sheep-pens" because they each had a door and benches surrounding the enclosure. In 1866, the new pews were constructed to face north and no longer featured doors nor necessitated sitting with one's back to the minister.

After 1866, the north gallery, which originally united the east and west galleries, was removed and east and west were reconstructed. At the same time, the upper tier of windows was lowered by two feet, and a cast-iron stove was installed. Stovepipes ran under the newly configured galleries.

Dorus Clarke, minister from 1823 to 1835, was born north of Blandford in Westhampton, Massachusetts, in 1797. Educated at Williams College and the Andover Theological Seminary, Clarke was ordained at Blandford on February 5, 1823, thus becoming the first full-time minister to serve in the White Church. Reverend Clarke went on to a distinguished career, serving in Chicopee Falls, Springfield, Massachusetts, following his time in Blandford. Between 1841 and the 1860s, Clarke served as editor of *New England Puritan*, *Christian Parlor Magazine*, *Christian Times*, and *Christian Alliance and Family Visitor*. In addition to publishing numerous essays, sermons, and tracts, Clarke was awarded an honorary doctor of divinity by his alma mater in 1868.

Charles J. Hinsdale was born in New York City in 1796. By 1800, his family had moved to Newark, New Jersey, and he graduated from Yale in 1815. Hinsdale also studied at Andover and Princeton seminaries, completing his work in 1819. After pursuing missionary work in the American South until 1822, Reverend Hinsdale was ordained in 1823 at the First Congregational Church of Meriden, Connecticut, where he remained for a decade. Hinsdale was installed at Blandford on January 20, 1836. Reverend Hinsdale served Blandford as the settled pastor from 1835 until 1860, then remained the part-time minister until 1863.

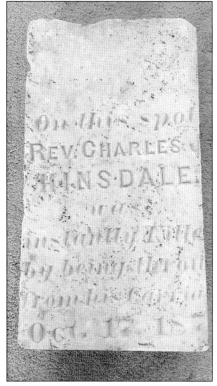

Reverend Hinsdale remained in Blandford after retirement and the death of his first wife, Catherine, in 1865. In mid-October 1871, Hinsdale was instantly killed when he was thrown from his horse-drawn carriage. This stone marker, now in the White Church, remained at the site of his death for years.

This double bass, also sometimes referred to as the American bass viol, New England bass viol, or Yankee bass viol, was used in churches to provide a consistent key to the singers in Congregational churches. The congregation purchased this double bass in Boston, most likely directly from the manufacturer, Henry Prentiss, who made musical instruments and umbrellas as well as printing sheet music at his shop on Court Street.

Gordon C. Rowley stands with the congregation's bass viol. The instrument was six feet, eleven inches with one-quarter-inch-diameter strings. The bass viol was purchased around 1843 as the congregation desired to add music to assist the choir. At various times between 1843 and 1855, the bass viol was played by Orin Carter, Lucius Bishop, and Chancy S. Brown. Brown taught Rowley how to play the instrument, and the latter recalled needing to stand on a stool to reach the fingerboard. Rowley never played it in church but kept the instrument in good condition from about 1880 until 1894.

In 1858, the congregation of the White Church purchased a harmonium melodeon, which was used until the meetinghouse was remodeled between 1865 and 1867. Former Blandford resident Orrin Sage helped raise funds to purchase what became known as the Johnson organ, manufactured in nearby Westfield by the William A. Johnson Organ Company. This image has long been labeled as Catherine Hinsdale, wife of Rev. Charles J. Hinsdale, playing the organ, but she died in 1865.

Interior, Congregational Church—BLANDFORD
From Photo by Mr. Arthur Ware

In 1910, Dr. W.H. Deane donated a pipe organ to replace the Johnson model, which had been moved to the winter chapel, a short walk from the White Church. Renovation had to be conducted in order to fit the organ, so an extension stood off the north wall until 1938, when the organ was removed.

This is possibly Rev. Aaron W. Field, who served as pastor from 1872 until 1879. Reverend Field moved on to Agawam by 1880, continuing his life as a clergyman with his wife, Jennie, and three children, Arthur, Alice, and Wesley. Reverend Field passed away in Gilsum, New Hampshire, in 1922 at the age of 84.

This White Church minister's identity is a mystery. In some measure, it is easier to identify who he is not: a process of elimination indicates that he could be Rev. B.F. Manwell, who briefly served the church from 1870 to 1871. Markings on the reverse side of the photograph indicate the image was made at the Westfield, Massachusetts, studios of Thomas P. Collins, who died in 1872. Reverend Manwell was from Androscoggin County, Maine.

Rev. Theodore Leete was born in Guilford, Connecticut, in 1814. Reverend Leete attended Yale, completing his initial studies in 1839 and graduating from Yale Theological Seminary in 1843. Leete was pastor at the First Church in Windsor, Connecticut, from 1845 to 1859, marrying Mary Cooley White in 1851. Reverend Leete served in Blandford from 1865 until 1870, dying in Longmeadow, Massachusetts, in 1886.

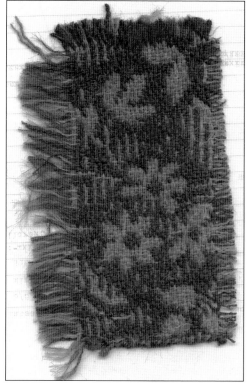

This carpet was installed in the White Church in 1884 at a cost of $279.26, including shipping and installation. The church took the carpet up off the floor in 1957 after 73 years of service. In 1984, the swatch had purpose again after Doris W. Hayden placed it into a section of the church records.

Rev. Allan C. Ferrin was minister from 1896 until 1901. Born in Vermont in 1860, by 1902 Reverend Ferrin, his wife, and two sons had returned north when he took the job of pastor of the Congregational church in Springfield, Vermont. It was a brief stay, as he journeyed on to serve as pastor in Lowell, Massachusetts, and, by 1920, performed interdenominational church work in Springfield, Massachusetts.

# Four

# The White Church in the 20th Century

## 1900–1980s

The congregation of the White Church built a winter chapel in the early 20th century a short five-minute walk down the hill from Damon's church. With its construction, the stoves were removed from the White Church, and the congregation used the building only in the warmer months of the year. By 1920, the Johnson organ, originally installed in the White Church, was moved to the winter chapel, where it remains.

At about the same time, the town, with the aid of summer resident Dr. Plumb Brown of Springfield, Massachusetts, began to mark historic spots in Blandford. A monument committee, consisting of Dr. Brown, Enos Boise, and Rev. Sumner G. Wood, held a brief service in July 1903 to unveil a boulder with an inscribed bronze tablet marking the location of Blandford's original meetinghouse (see chapter one for image).

Even as the congregation removed itself from the building for a portion of the year, the White Church remained an important symbol of the town and was a draw for postcard manufacturers and other artists. Representations of Blandford were not seen as complete if they did not include the White Church.

In 1907, the decision was reached to install a metal ceiling in the White Church. H.J. Porter was paid $529.73 for this work as well as redoing some of the plaster on side walls. Half a century later, a redecorating committee approved interior work on the White Church.

In the 250th year of Blandford's existence, the White Church was accepted in the National Register of Historic Places. This effort was aided by work from Connecticut Valley Preservation Services, a consulting firm in Southwick, Massachusetts, and the Massachusetts Historical Commission, the latter of which formally nominated the White Church for consideration. With its placement in the register, the White Church joined another of Isaac Damon's creations, the First Congregational Church of Springfield, Massachusetts, which was placed in the register in 1972.

This recognition was seen as essential in raising funds for much needed repairs for both the exterior and interior of the church. In 1985, the thought was the congregation would require at least $30,000 to straighten the foundation and replace the sill plate (wooden foundation), which was rotting. In the end, the White Church would require more care, more repair, and many more dollars to fulfill its restoration.

In this late-19th-century image of the White Church, residents can be seen gathered in front in horse-drawn carriages. On the north roof, a chimney whose stove helped provide heat can be observed.

Rev. Sumner G. Wood served for 10 years as pastor of both the First Congregational Church and the Congregational parish in North Blandford, from 1901 to 1911. Wood was, in a way, returning, as Blandford was home to his paternal grandmother of seven generations back. Like other ministers of the community, Wood was a Williams College graduate.

An early postcard features the White Church. This image from 1905 was taken at cattle show time and was mailed to William Bartlett of Feeding Hills from Maude.

FIRST CONGREGATIONAL CHURCH
BLANDFORD, MASS.

Postcard production was taking off in the early 20th century, and this particular card is one such example. Printed by the Allied Printing Trades Council of Waukegan, Illinois, it was in some ways unusual, as many American and Canadian cards of the era were printed in Germany to be sold in the United States.

The Old Burying
Ground

BLANDFORD

These postcards were a way of both preserving the history of a place and telling a story to people. The Old Burying Ground of Blandford, pictured here prior to 1910, shows many pine trees having grown up among the headstones. In the late 1990s, these pines were cut down.

CONGREGATIONAL CHURCH, BLANDFORD, MASS.

The Blandford Historical Society has several versions of this particular postcard, including hand-tinted images. The focus on the church is easy to achieve here, looking from the south to northeast.

GONGREGATIONAL CHURCH          BLANDFORD, MASS.

This card was produced prior to 1907. On cards made between 1901 and 1907, senders were not permitted to write messages on the address side by order of the postmaster general. Note the chimney on the north roof.

The Old Meeting House Blandford
[*First Congregational Church*]
Built 1822.

This card was also produced prior to 1907 with no space for a message on the reverse. It is curiously labeled "The Old Meeting House," which is a somewhat inaccurate statement, given that the old meetinghouse had been dismantled.

CONGREGATIONAL CHURCH ON THE COMMON, BLANDFORD MASS.
W. J. PEEBLES' SERIES

*will be I suppose you will be in Boston you will be givn. Mabel.*

This card was produced prior to 1907 but not mailed to Burt Hunt in Springfield until 1909, after the transition to allow messages on the address side. However, the writer followed the rules of the production year of the card, writing her message on the front beneath the image of the White Church atop the hill.

15820

1st Congregational Church
Blandford, Mass.
Elevation 1500 Ft.

The Dexter Press of Pearl River, New York, produced this card featuring the White Church. The elevation of the hill on which the church sits was emphasized as well.

THE
CONGREGATIONAL
CHURCH

BLANDFORD

This card was produced after the transition to the divided back, so writers were able to identify a space for their message as well as a space for the address on the reverse side. The winter scene featuring a horse-drawn sleigh heading toward the White Church captures snow on the pines and the road.

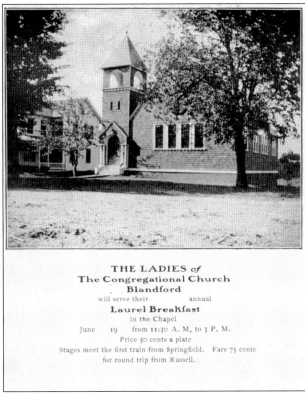

THE LADIES of
The Congregational Church
Blandford
will serve their            annual
Laurel Breakfast
in the Chapel
June    19    from 11:30 A. M. to 3 P. M.
Price 50 cents a plate
Stages meet the first train from Springfield.   Fare 75 cents
for round trip from Russell.

By the early 1900s, the congregation had built a so-called winter chapel down the hill and to the east of the White Church. What little heating had existed in the White Church was removed, and the Johnson organ was placed in the newer chapel. The card reminds those interested to join one of the two ladies' societies in Blandford for the annual breakfast in mid-June. The parsonage for the minister can be seen at left.

North Street and the Fair Grounds           BLANDFORD

This image, taken from the steeple of the White Church, focuses on the Blandford fairgrounds to the north. Mailed in August 1911, the message reads, "I sent the pears by freight so if they don't come soon you will have to phone to Westfield and see where they are. Mother."

BIRD'S EYE VIEW, BLANDFORD, MASS.

This card was produced by P. Masters of Riverton, Connecticut, after 1920. Also taken from the church steeple, the lens focuses east and slightly south, capturing Deane Memorial Building, constructed following the death of benefactor Dr. Wallace Deane.

The Dr. Dean Memorial Building, Blandford, Mass.

Mailed in August 1929, this E.J. Curtis postcard features the Deane Memorial Building, which served as a home for secondary education for Blandford residents for about two decades.

Dean Memorial Park, Blandford, Mass.

The E.J. Curtis store of photography in Pittsfield, Massachusetts, produced this card. Deane Memorial Hall is at left along with a park featuring flowers, a gazebo, and more, while the White Church is seen through the trees to the right.

Church Hill, Blandford, Mass.

Another E.J. Curtis postcard captures "church hill," yet the White Church itself is missing. At left stands the building that today serves as the headquarters for the Blandford Historical Society.

Rev. Irving Childs served as minister of the church from 1918 to 1920. He is pictured here with his wife, Lizzie. The couple had five children and rented a home on Main Street in Blandford during their short tenure in town.

Orrin Sage House

Orrin Sage moved to Blandford in 1811 and played a significant role in the economic development of the town in the early 19th century. Even after moving from Blandford to Ware, Massachusetts, Sage remained connected, helping to raise funds for the purchase of the Johnson organ, which still stands in what became known as the winter chapel for the congregation. This 20th-century rendition of Sage and his home was done by artist Mary MacDonnell.

In this eastern view taken in 1935 from the belfry of the White Church, the buildings of Blandford's Main Street are clearly laid out. The other church visible in the center distance is the now-demolished Methodist church.

This image at the intersection of Main and North Streets was taken in 1935 and focuses on the schoolhouse that became the home of the Blandford Historical Society. The White Church is barely visible through the pine trees to the north.

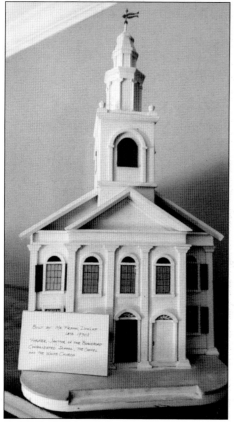

The White Church inspired many artists and photographers over the years. This beautiful birdhouse was constructed after artist Frank Dunlap spent a year working with 12-year-old Blandford resident Edward Cady, who won first prize at the 1937 Blandford fair in the arts and crafts division with his version of the birdhouse.

Frank Dunlap, custodian at the Blandford Consolidated School, the chapel, and the White Church, assisted young Edward Cady with his birdhouse construction. Dunlap helped any students interested in woodworking projects during recess time at the school and provided tools and guidance. He enjoyed working with Cady so much he made his own version of the White Church birdhouse, which sits in the Blandford Historical Society.

As part of Pres. Franklin Roosevelt's New Deal programs, the Historic American Buildings Survey (HABS) began after 1933. Teams of photographers and architects created images and sketches of important buildings throughout the United States. The White Church was captured sometime after 1941. The church was considered to be a well-preserved example of the Federal-style New England meetinghouse. (Courtesy of Library of Congress.)

The HABS team photographed the exterior and interior of historic buildings like the White Church. This shot was taken from the northwest looking back at the rear of the church. Architect Isaac Damon's five-over-five window pattern is repeated on the west and east sides of the church but not the north. On the south side (or front facing), Damon used a variation on the five-over-five pattern, with five windows above two windows and three doorways. (Courtesy of Library of Congress.)

This view of the White Church sanctuary looks from south to north. At the time this image was taken, the church was still the summer meetinghouse for the First Congregational Church of Blandford. Against the north wall, a Hammond organ, procured in the mid- to late 1930s, is slightly visible. The church was around 120 years old when the photograph was taken, and some wear and damage is visible on both the walls and the tin ceiling. (Courtesy of Library of Congress.)

This photograph taken from the north looks from the pulpit toward the south end of the worship space. The vestibule and stairs leading up to seating on the second-floor lofts are both visible, as is a portrait of Rev. Charles J. Hinsdale (minister, 1835–1863) and a bass viol, which was purchased by the congregation around 1843. While the south view reveals slightly less damage, some cracks can be observed on the plaster walls near the entry doors to the galleys on the second floor. (Courtesy of Library of Congress.)

The congregation's winter chapel, also referred to as the village church, included a kitchen and dining area that were redone in late 1949. Photographs were sent to a Blandford resident, Beulah Lee Wyman, in early February 1950 from home demonstration agent Molly M. Higgins of the cooperative extension in agriculture and home economics for the State of Massachusetts.

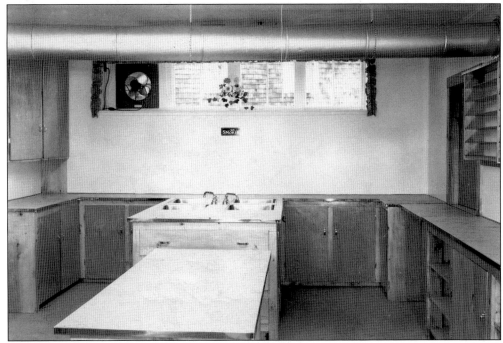

The kitchen featured a gas range with two ovens, a double sink, ample food preparation areas, and "pie shelves" (seen above the counter at right) on which to hold small plates with desserts.

Several passways connected the kitchen to the dining area, which was remodeled at the same time as the kitchen. At left, a serving window can be viewed. At right, a half door opened to allow easy transfer of soiled dishes to the sinks for cleanup.

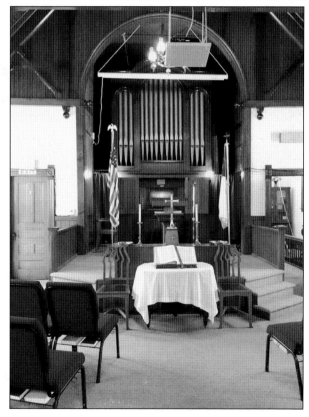

The Johnson organ, originally installed in the White Church, was moved to the winter chapel in the early 20th century. The organ's placement behind the pulpit in the winter chapel differs from its position behind congregants when it was in the White Church. (Photograph by Pliny Norcross III.)

Rev. Edwin A. Crocker of Canada served as minister from 1952 to 1964. Interestingly, 12 years earlier, Crocker worked as the pastor of a Methodist church in Milo, Maine.

Rev. Brian Care was the minister from 1983 to 1991. Pictured here inside the White Church, Reverend Care helped get the church into the National Register of Historic Places.

In celebration of 250 years of Blandford, town residents crafted a quilt that highlighted historical events in the town's existence, including the passing of Gen. Henry Knox on his way to Boston from Ticonderoga in 1775. The agricultural history of the community, education, and historic homes were represented as well. The White Church served as the centerpiece for the commemorative quilt.

The White Church

In the bicentennial year, 1976, artist Mary MacDonnell was asked to draw pen-and-ink images of historic homes in Blandford. While MacDonnell's work largely focused on houses, the White Church was a natural target.

*Five*

# THE WHITE CHURCH PRESERVED
## 1990–2003

After raising the church on steel I-beams in order to rebuild the foundation, the initial restoration efforts of the damaged building faltered, and the White Church would remain suspended above the hilltop for nearly three years. From May through July 1993, masonry was completed, and a new front porch was built. At the same time, the sills were replaced, a vapor barrier was added to the crawlspace, and a handicapped exit was created for the north side of the church.

Upon completion of the roof and window repairs, teams shifted to renovations of the interior of the building in the spring of 1994. All the while, myriad fundraising efforts continued. In the summer of 1994, the White Church Restoration Committee worked to develop a fundraising event that harkened back to the Scots heritage of the community. In late July, the former Glasgow Lands hosted a Scottish festival on the Blandford fairgrounds that included Highland dancing, athletic games, sheep-herding demonstrations, piping bands, Scottish livestock, and a calling of the clans. The Blandford Historical Society ran a tearoom in the agricultural hall, and spinners and weavers worked in the arts building.

In 1995, a summer resident of Blandford, Eve Queler, embraced the church restoration fundraising efforts, bringing what became known as the Bel Canto singers to Blandford for a performance every summer. All profits from these concerts went to the White Church, and ultimately, the Bel Canto performances were responsible for approximately $200,000 over a 25-year period. Although unable to perform in 2020, the Bel Canto singers made a return to the White Church in late August 2021.

Sally D. Grugan's zoom view of the bell tower, steeple, and weather vane was one the photographer played with frequently in the 1990s. Though this image is a standard photograph, she sometimes printed negative versions, focused on the entire church, or aimed her camera at specific sections, documenting the building as it hit 170 years plus.

Even as the White Church needed repair, it remained a draw for artists. In the background, some contractors' trucks can be seen in front of the church.

Pictured at right is the White Church as portrayed by artist Beranese Fowler. This painting features the National Register of Historic Places tablet and the new front steps.

Pictured above is the White Church as portrayed by artist Edward Mead. The pine trees remain prominent in the artist's vision to the left as the rise of the hill leading to the church is emphasized, somewhat obscuring the porch.

Artist Muriel Ritchie created this painting of the White Church. It was given to the Blandford Historical Society in memory of residents Natalie and Ted Couse. Natalie Couse lived to be 103 years old.

The White Church had fallen into severe disrepair by the 1980s. The floorboards at the front entrance, symptomatic of larger issues, were pulling away or rotting through at the edges of the rounded porch.

The congregation raised funds to renovate the church. First Congregational pastor Brian Care (left) watches while Don Christian Jr. (center) aids contractor Rick Moraweic (right) with the ceremonial ground-breaking shovels on April 22, 1990.

Trumpeter Jason Horne played at the April 1990 ceremony on the steps of the White Church. The deck and stairs would eventually be rebuilt.

Numerous contributors have had an influence on repairing the damaged church since 1990. Historic Preservation Associates, architect Harry Pisila, Rick Moraweic, Florido Testa, and Lee Hamburg are all acknowledged on these signs.

Tom Ackley of Blandford excavated the foundation of the White Church. This process was essential for accessing the rotting sill.

When Tom Ackley's work was completed, the area surrounding the foundation was accessible. In addition to assessing damage, the excavation work cleared the way for the next step in the reconstruction process.

With excavation completed, the White Church could now be jacked up and set on I-beams. Hicks Building Movers of Brimfield, Massachusetts, conducted this part of the operation.

The height to which the church was raised is visible in this image. An excavator continues to clean out underneath the church.

The southwest corner of the church is visible in this image. The rubble and dirt from excavation is evident.

The front porch was stripped away, and the church was jacked up to be placed on steel I-beams. The crumbling foundation would require full replacement to sustain the weight of the building as reconstruction continued.

By June 1990, several steps had been undertaken, including excavation, assessment of the foundation, some masonry work, and the replacement of the church's sills. The bill had already hit nearly $47,000.

The White Church seemed to be suspended above the ground, precariously tilting slightly to the north and west. From this angle, the pine trees continued to provide a unique framing of the building.

Taken from a different angle, the raising is somewhat muted. At this point, the congregation had already expended nearly $47,000 and ran short of funds, so the church would remain in this state for three years.

In 1992, Ann Southworth offered to help raise additional funds, and in 1993, the restoration project resumed with a team that included the following: architect Harry Pisila, contractor Florido Testa, and historic preservationist Peter Hamm. Ann Southworth, pictured at left, was supported by cochair Sumner Robbins (center) and treasurer Sarah "Sally" Robbins (right). The team needed to raise an estimated $250,000 to complete the goals of the White Church Restoration Committee.

In 1994, Westfield Bank donated $5,000 to the restoration effort. Accepting the check from Westfield Bank are cochair Sumner Robbins (left) and treasurer Sarah "Sally" Robbins (center).

The White Church bell was cast by G.H. Holbrook of Medway, Massachusetts, in 1835. A massive 18-inch-by-16-inch timber supports the floor underneath the bell in the enclosed belfry.

After agreeing to serve as cochair for the White Church Restoration Committee, Sumner Robbins climbed into the steeple to capture this image looking east. At center right, the city of Springfield, Massachusetts, is visible in the distance.

Still raised on I-beams, the White Church required both interior and exterior repairs. On the north side of the church (rear), the faint outline of construction work done in the 19th century can be seen.

Years of paint would need to be examined and removed before additional repairs could be made. The close-up of a window here reveals the cracking of the aged paint.

The interior held more damage. As with other locations in the church, the cracking and peeling, already a challenge with age, had been exacerbated by the raising of the church to rework the foundation.

Removing debris from the basement and setting up to complete masonry was key to getting the church off the I-beams. This portion of the project began in early May 1993 and continued until July of that year.

Foundation work on the east side of the church required a lot of replacement and build up before the I-beams could be scheduled for removal. Above the worker, bracers are visible on two of the windows.

Another view of the east side of the building was taken looking to the north. Props were installed that would later be replaced with a stone base.

As the foundation was built up, the steel beams could still be seen. Also note the wood under the foundation line along the wall.

The rebuilt space of the foundation can be seen here. This image contains props for sills that would be replaced with a stone base.

Sumner Robbins took this photograph of the southwest corner of the church. With snow still on the ground, plans were being laid to complete foundation repairs.

The sill plate to be replaced can be viewed here. The snow stuck around into late March in 1993.

The sill plate to be replaced can be viewed. By early May, the snow was gone, and work could now proceed in earnest.

The east wall basement entrance with the prop removed is visible here. The sill has been replaced and elements of the foundation are being built up.

As the wooden sills were replaced, vents for the crawlspace were installed. Debris and material needed to be hauled out, and fill needed to be smoothed and flattened.

A mylar plastic vapor barrier was installed. Sand had been distributed and smoothed underneath the newly established foundation.

On the east side of the church, the steel beams have been removed. The pile of stone in the foreground was intended to be used for the foundation facing.

At the northwest corner of the church, Blandford residents helped the project to completion. Here, Arthur Wyman Jr. (left) splits stones for the foundation facing while Arthur Wyman Sr. (right) watches.

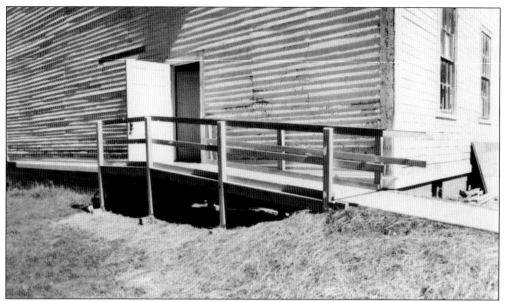

With the foundation reconstructed and the base of the church solid, another needed addition was installed. On the north side of the church, close to where a wall had once been opened up to fit the organ installed in 1910, an accessible entry and exit was assembled.

In mid-July 1993, a series of roof repairs were undertaken. The surface was wire brushed and then painted.

The roof repairs were lengthy, continuing until mid-October 1993. This high off the ground, safety lines are an absolute necessity.

This image captures the damage done to the cornice on the southwest side of the church; all surfaces had to be scraped and painted. The crew also installed terne-coated stainless steel drip edges all along the roof to minimize water washing down the front of the building.

As this Sumner Robbins photograph captures, the church still required rebuilding of the steps. This process was completed after the foundation work.

Blandford resident Steve Hart was called upon to aid in the project. Hart excavated the area required for installing the new porch and steps.

Florido Testa, builders from Hillsdale, New York, constructed the porch and steps. Here, the team works to get the foundations for the new stairs level.

The carpentry work for the front porch risers was underway by late spring. This part of the project was largely completed in June 1993.

The stringers for the stairs are pictured here settling into their new home. With the stringers level and the porch taking shape, regular access to the church was soon reestablished.

With the front porch completed, it was time to engage in some treatment on the wood. The stringers still await their steps at this point in the process.

By late June 1993, the exterior of the church was taking shape. Work had commenced on the upper windows, the deck and steps were installed, and new railings were in place.

In what was termed the third phase of the renovation project, the window sash required extensive work. This south-side window was photographed in September 1993 revealing the general condition of the exterior sash.

There were some windows that exhibited a worst-case scenario. In this case, all the panes would have to be replaced and elements of the window would require rebuilding. This image also captures the extent to which the exterior paint would require work.

Many windows were passable but required new panes of glass. Visible at left are lightning grounds that run from the roofline to the base of the church.

As the windows were awaiting final replacements in late December 1993 and early January 1994, it was time to consider the interior repairs. The southwest side of the building here reveals plywood blocking off the window and hints at more needed work.

In the south wall, cracks became apparent. The space under the balcony also revealed rusting in the areas in which tin had been installed.

In the north wall, just behind the pulpit area, the damage was more severe. The archway lathing is almost completely visible, and rust stains wash down the walls.

In this southeast corner, a variety of levels of wear and tear were discovered. Missing plaster, broken lathes, and water damage would all require attention.

The damage was not confined to the walls and windows. With myriad broken window panes and other entrance opportunities, birds had made the White Church their home, damaging pews and upholstery.

The tin ceiling was rusting in multiple locations. While cleaning could mitigate some of the damage, in some instances the rust had all but destroyed the pieces installed in the early 20th century.

In instances where the tin had to be replaced, molds would be cast in order to replicate the design. This piece was cast from details in the existing ceiling, enabling replacement pieces to look like the original.

Between April 1 and July 6, 1994, reconstruction work was focused on interior repairs. The tin ceiling had been installed in 1907 to cover the original plaster. Here, workers erected staging to reach the tin, wire brushed and repaired the ceiling, created plaster castings of deteriorated areas, and then painted the ceiling and trim.

In some instances, the work undertaken to save the structure had created additional damage. In the upper balcony along the west wall, cracks under the windows emerged as a result of jacking up the building to replace the foundation.

Once the molds were completed, the tin roof was mostly repaired. However, scaffolding had to be assembled in order to complete the painting of the roof, including the intricate detailing.

The south wall and ceiling, along with the eastern balcony, are revealed in this image. Not all pieces of the ceiling had to be recast, but every space required cleaning and repainting.

As the repairs proceeded, fascinating overlaps between old and new were revealed. Here, a juncture between the new casted ceiling panel and the original demonstrates the care with which the ceiling was repaired.

This image was taken atop scaffolding toward the southern portion of the building looking to the northwest. The freshly painted walls and ceiling gleam.

When the tin ceiling was originally installed, several beautifully detailed sections were added to give dimension to the surfaces. The central rosette is one such example with its flourishes of leaves, columns, and flames painted white and augmented with gold highlights.

From the center of the rosette hangs a light fixture. Cracks in the plaster and in the northern archway were effectively repaired, and the new paint fairly shines as it reflects the light streaming in from the windows.

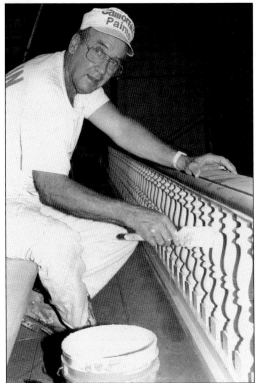

Don Hamlin of Brimfield, Massachusetts, pauses in his work at the balcony levels. All the railings required fresh coats of paint.

This is a reminder of all the work that had been completed. While this photograph taken by Sumner Robbins reveals the newly repaired windows to the east, it also shows the damage to the interior walls, which was repaired in the spring and summer of 1994.

Fundraising efforts continued even as the restoration work was underway. This quilt was raffled to benefit the church and sold tickets worth $1,288 at the Glasgow Lands Scottish Festival in the summer of 1994.

Quilters present the check to Ann Southworth (far right). The artisans who created the quilt are, from left to right, Barbar Boulay, Cheryl Hopson, Sue Racine, Ruth Lapris, Helen Barnoski, and Agnes Cook.

In the early fall of 1993, before all of the windows had been fixed, Blandford's Pat Lucas captured this image of the White Church on its way to restoration. While the front deck and stair reconstruction is complete and the roof improved, the building still had more work to come. However, the promise was visible.

By the summer of 1994, with window sash at the ready and plaster walls repaired, painted, and more, the White Church was ready to host one the first of a series of Scottish festivals and fairs that would provide needed revenue for further restoration work.

To celebrate the Scots heritage of the town, Pat Lucas, Mary MacDonnell, Helen Barnoski, Ruth LaPrise, Charlotte Smith, Co Cousineau, Kim Blanchette, Brenda Blood, and Raymah Wojick crafted replica Scots flags. One of the flags flies in the foreground from a telephone pole located to the south of the White Church.

Kate Lovejoy holds one of the St. Andrew's flags that were crafted to sell for the benefit of the White Church restoration fund. The midnight blue flag with a white St. Andrew's cross was priced at $15.

Sheila Lucas performs the Highland sword dance at the first festival, hosted on July 30, 1994. The festival would draw dancers from across the Northeast and eventually include competitions.

Games and competitions were part of the festival, which raised over $13,000 for the White Church (seen in the background) restoration fund. The sheaf toss, in which a burlap sack filled with straw is tossed with a pitchfork, is pictured here.

Scots livestock, including Highland cattle, were on display. These hardy creatures from the Highlands and Outer Hebrides islands of Scotland likely were not brought to Blandford by its early Scots inhabitants.

A Scots *dunface* or Old Scottish short wool sheep is pictured above. These were sometimes hybrids of Shetland and Hebridean sheep.

The Kiltie Band of Springfield, Massachusetts, performed at the festival. The White Church steeple is visible in the background.

Established in 1917, the Kiltie Band of Springfield, Massachusetts, is one of the oldest pipe bands in the United States. The band was founded by Jack MacGregor, who came to Massachusetts from Aberdeen, Scotland.

The White Church hosted many events during the Scottish festival as well. Here, Julie MacNayr Pike of Montgomery, Massachusetts, sings.

Eric Goodchild performs on violin in the pulpit of the White Church. Michael Batura plays the harp.

Robert Tunnicliffe of Lanesboro, Massachusetts, recites Robert Burns poetry during the festival. The newly restored main audience room in front of the pulpit area gleams behind Tunnicliffe.

Having experienced financial success in 1994, the community repeated the festival in the summer of 1995. Here, Maureen Costello (right) of Blandford spins while explaining the process to a festival attendee.

Barbara Blair of Blandford works the spinning wheel in 1995. The second Glasgow Lands Scottish Festival featured not only crafts like spinning but also a tearoom, vendors with Scottish foods, and representatives from 16 different clans.

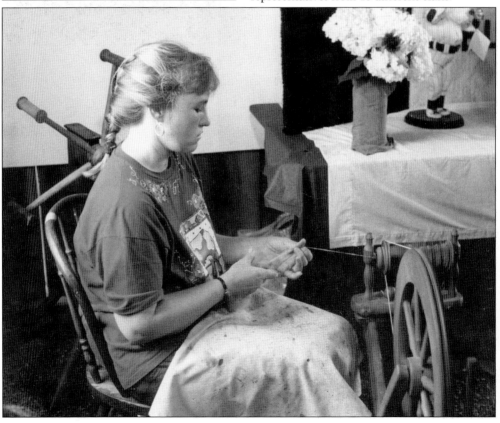

As the festival evolved and continued to raise money for the White Church, more participants joined. This 74th Highland Regiment of Foot reenactor stands before his tent in 1997. The church steeple is seen far to the back left.

Historic Highlanders are armed to the teeth at the festival in 1997. This nonprofit educational organization was founded in 1989 with members from across New England.

As the festival evolved and continued to raise money for the White Church, more events were added. The church is visible in the background of these armored jousting competitors.

The jousting and much of the festival was originally hosted at the Blandford fairgrounds behind the White Church. With the church's steeple visible in the background, these combatants clashed in 1998.

Perhaps a portend of the future, the Hale–Bopp comet can be seen in the night sky over the White Church. Restoration committee cochair Sumner Robbins captured the comet on April 7, 1997, probably around 9:00 p.m. Astronomy and physics professor Dr. Rick Rees of Westfield State University was able to calculate the date and the approximate time of Robbins's photograph using a specialized planetarium computer program.

By the summer of 1997, the White Church restoration had consumed in excess of $285,000. The congregation and the White Church Restoration Committee continued fundraising efforts, including holding concerts. In this image, a rented grand piano is moved up the renovated porch in early August 1997 for an evening opera performance.

In the late summer of 1997, the White Church had a dedication ceremony that included scripture readings, a homily from Pastor Ed Lewis, and talks from Ann Southworth and Sumner Robbins on the efforts made by the community to restore the building. While there was still additional work remaining, this image from the early winter of 1997 encompasses much of the completed exterior repairs.

Interior work in the roofing and steeple area remained on the agenda. This image at the ridge pole of the roof reveals a reminder of the former stovepipes that once passed through the ceiling.

The stove had been in the center of the sanctuary. In 1998, patches were placed over the former locations where the metal pipes ran through the ceiling to enter a central chimney.

When a stove was placed in the sanctuary in each southern corner in 1866, the pipes connected with chimneys in the north wall. The two chimneys that remained by the late 1990s were finally removed.

Throughout the 1990s, photographer Sally D. Grugan captured the White Church from a variety of angles. Grugan was a member of the Photographic Society of America for 40 years and won numerous awards for her photography. A collection of her photographs is held at the Blandford Historical Society.

# *Six*

# THE WHITE CHURCH AS COMMUNITY SPACE

## 2003–PRESENT

The Blandford Historical Society was incorporated in 1935. In the 1990s, the historical society aided in the initial preservation efforts for the White Church, and the society maintains an investment fund with the purpose of financing repairs and maintenance on the White Church. In 2006, the Congregational Church sold the White Church to the Blandford Historical Society for $1. This transition supported concentrated efforts to help preserve Blandford's only building in the National Register of Historic Places.

The Blandford Historical Society and the Congregational Church have sponsored a variety of events at the White Church. Examples include the Blandford Summer Concert series, partially supported by regional Massachusetts Cultural Councils; gospel singers invited by the Congregational Church; and Mennonite singers who use the White Church as a starting point for a 10-location tour.

To keep the White Church in shape, renovation is a consistent need. After the initial push in the 1990s to return the building to usable shape, regular maintenance has been possible because of the commitment from both the Blandford Historical Society and the community.

In 2020, anticipating the 200th anniversary of the church's construction, the Blandford Historical Society applied for and received a substantial grant from the Massachusetts Cultural Council Capital Fund. Pliny "Chips" Norcross, president of the Blandford Historical Society, was the grant writer and onsite clerk of the works. The project aimed to work on four main points: the renovation and repainting of the steeple, the restoring of the building's 25 windows, the painting of the building's exterior, and the repair of cracks in the plaster walls as well as painting of the interior.

Peter Hamm, the founder of Historic Preservation Associates in Wales, Massachusetts, has been associated with the White Church for over two decades. Committed to protecting the architectural history of New England, Peter Hamm has been an ideal partner in the longstanding White Church restoration efforts.

While Hamm served as general contractor, Don Hayward of Greenfield, Massachusetts, performed the window restoration, and Trafford Painting of Brimfield, Massachusetts, worked on exterior and interior painting. Finally, minor cracks and other plaster repair was conducted by Ray Crane. Because of COVID-19, the 2020 concert series was canceled, so these restoration and maintenance efforts were accomplished without interruption.

Efforts to preserve the White Church continue, and grants such as that from the Massachusetts Cultural Council Capital Fund are only a part of the story. Individuals are still making donations, while continued support comes from state representative Smitty Pignatelli, the Blandford Board of Selectmen, elders of the First Congregational Church of Blandford, and the Board of Library Trustees of Blandford.

As typical of many Christian churches, the White Church included a prominent steeple. A continual process in restoration involves inspection to determine whether structural damage or water infiltration has occurred. This photograph taken in the mid-1990s during an inspection captures the top of the White Church steeple from the inside.

Inside the belfry, evidence persists of many visitors to the higher spaces of the structure. This image demonstrates how visitors have carved or written initials and dates ranging from the late 1800s to the 1950s.

At various times during restoration, complex scaffolding has been established around the church to work on elements of the steeple and facing. This image was taken during what was termed phase three of the restoration in 1994. In 2020, similar scaffolding necessary for the steeple work was reinstalled under the direction of Ken Boudreau from the Marr Scaffolding Company in nearby Springfield, Massachusetts.

In some of the original repairs, work focused on touching up the exterior of the steeple and the cupola. The cupola, largely an ornamentation included by architect Isaac Damon, sits nestled in scaffolding in 1994.

In 2016, repairs were made to the interior and exterior of the steeple area. In this case, safety harnesses were attached inside by steeplejack Mark Paley and used to get outside to the spaces in need of repair. More carving and graffiti are visible on the timbers of the steeple.

Lowering himself to the deck below the pinnacle of the steeple, Mark Paley's task was to replace the four finials. These finials were greatly deteriorated, and their replacements were turned on a lathe from single blocks of wood. While completing this work, it was deemed necessary to renovate and repaint the steeple and regild the weather vane. The Blandford Historical Society applied for a grant to help this process along with the restoration of the church's 25 windows, repainting the exterior, and repairing cracks to the plaster walls on the inside with a repainting for the interior as well. The aim was to complete these various repairs in time for the 200th anniversary of the White Church's construction in 2022.

Peter Hamm runs Historic Preservation Associates of Wales, Massachusetts. Hamm has been associated with repairs for the White Church since the 1990s and was available as the general contractor for the latest set of repairs conducted in 2020 and 2021. Historic Preservation Associates has worked on historic house museums and private residences as well. Hamm helped direct projects at the Emily Dickinson house in Amherst, Massachusetts; Herman Melville's Arrowhead estate in Pittsfield, Massachusetts; and other locations.

The weather vane was regilded in 2020 by Huntington, Massachusetts, artist Jodi Simmons. For over 20 years, Simmons has been creating contemporary icon art, encompassing the use of handcrafted gold leaf application and embossing. Her extensive work with gilding made Simmons a perfect artist to restore the vane.

Components of the weather vane were set into place in 2020. The workers established a scaffold above the top of the steeple near the tip of the spire in order to position the repaired components.

Years before the repairs of the 2010s, this painting captures the position of the White Church and features some of the noted repairs. Three of the finials that were replaced in 2016 are visible above the bell tower as is the weather vane atop the spire.

The White Church remains a target of photographers who seek to capture a classic New England meetinghouse. Blandford resident Pamela Rideout took this photograph of the White Church from the east inside Watson Park, looking toward the west.

The White Church is pictured under scattered clouds and viewed from the southwest. This image captures three of the four repaired finials and the newly gilded weather vane.

The front of the White Church is viewed from the south. Isaac Damon's original design has been sharpened by a variety of restorations. Most arresting in this image are the windows and transoms over the three entrances.

The Wyman family, beginning with William Horatio and Eliza Hanchett Wyman, settled in Blandford in the 1830s. Their 2017 extended family reunion brought back several generations to Blandford from across the United States. Many Wymans had attended services at the White Church throughout the years, and family members helped lead worship on Sunday. The next family reunion will coincide with the 200th anniversary of the White Church in 2022. (Courtesy of Gary Hart.)

The interior of the White Church is filled with members of the Wyman family during their 2017 reunion. Many members of the family attended the church, which served as a home for worship, weddings, and funerals. In 2017, the Wyman family used the interior as a meeting place and to display a 90-foot-long printout of the descendants of William Horatio and Eliza Hanchett Wyman. On the south wall, images of the church's ministers, some of whom served ancestors of the Wyman family, can be seen, including Rev. Charles Hinsdale (1835–1863). (Courtesy of Gary Hart.)

Efforts to preserve the White Church come from all elements of the Blandford community. Eve Queler, the director emerita of the Opera Orchestra of New York, began her Bel Canto Opera Concert series in July 1995. Queler, a summer resident of Blandford, has now led 26 concert performances in the church. Queler extols the building for its acoustics and the intimate nature of the church. All profits from these concerts have gone to the White Church restoration fund, and ultimately, the Bel Canto performance money and careful investment have been responsible for approximately $200,000 of the fundraising over a quarter-century.

The White Church has hosted numerous musical events over the past quarter-century. Although COVID-19 interrupted performances in 2020, several concerts were held in August 2021. Here, Jeff Gavioli (conducting in the hat by the center aisle) and his Bad News Jazz and Blues Orchestra, featuring vocalist Cindy Reed, perform swing and big band–inspired music on August 14, 2021. (Courtesy of Nicholas J. Aieta.)

The White Church is lit up at night during one of the 2021 summer concerts. Three Saturdays in August 2021, the White Church played host to jazz and blues, classical work performed by Herdís Guðmundsdóttir and Liam Kaplan, and the 26th annual Bel Canto Opera featuring young opera singers under music director emerita of Opera Orchestra of New York Eve Queler. (Courtesy of Nicholas J. Aieta.)

# BIBLIOGRAPHY

"Consolidated Church Records Concerning Church Organization, Church Buildings, Musical Instruments, etc." Doris W. Hayden Collection, Blandford Historical Society.
*Daily Hampshire Gazette.* "Capt. Isaac Damon." August 4, 1904.
Farber, Jessie Lie. *Early American Gravestones: The Farber Collection.* Worcester, MA: American Antiquarian Society and Visual Information, 1997.
Glasgow Lands Scottish Festival Collection, Blandford Historical Society.
King, Moses, ed. *King's Handbook of Springfield, Massachusetts.* Springfield, MA: James D. Gill, 1884.
Postcard Collection, Blandford Historical Society.
"Reconnaissance Survey Town Report, Blandford." Massachusetts Historical Commission, 1982.
Sally Grugan Collection, Blandford Historical Society.
Warner, Charles F., ed. *Picturesque Hamden.* Northampton, MA: Picturesque Publishing Company, 1892.
Weis, Frederick Lewis. *The Colonial Clergy and the Colonial Churches of New England.* Lancaster, MA: Society of the Descendants of the Colonial Clergy, 1936.
White Church Restoration Collection, Blandford Historical Society.
Wood, Sumner Gilbert. *Homes and Habits of Blandford.* Blandford, MA: 250th Anniversary Committee, 1985.
———. *The Taverns and Turnpikes of Blandford, 1733–1833.* Blandford, MA: self-published, 1908.

# About the Blandford Historical Society

The Blandford Historical Society was founded in 1935 as a nonprofit organization that promotes the study, preservation, and celebration of local history. Through the years, the society has acquired a substantial collection of artifacts, documents, and images, which is currently housed in our 1845 former central schoolhouse, owned by the town. Every Labor Day weekend, the society provides an exhibit in our building at the Blandford Agricultural Fair. The society also has extensive genealogical files, which are used by researchers from all across the country. Each year, the Blandford Historical Society offers a number of free programs to the general public on a wide variety of topics. In addition, it provides the community with a fundraising Blandford Summer Concerts series featuring a wide variety of music. Our facilities are open on special holidays, by appointment, and may also be rented for weddings, funerals, and other celebrations. The Blandford Historical Society can be reached at (413) 848-0108; PO Box 35, Blandford, Massachusetts, 01008; or thewhitechurch.org.

# DISCOVER THOUSANDS OF LOCAL HISTORY BOOKS
## FEATURING MILLIONS OF VINTAGE IMAGES

Arcadia Publishing, the leading local history publisher in the United States, is committed to making history accessible and meaningful through publishing books that celebrate and preserve the heritage of America's people and places.

## Find more books like this at
## www.arcadiapublishing.com

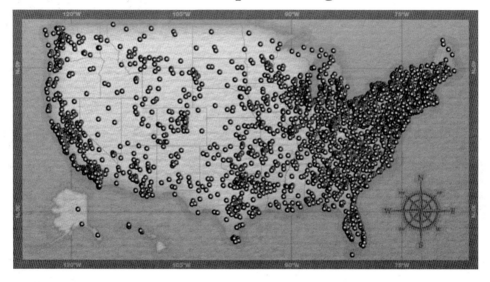

Search for your hometown history, your old stomping grounds, and even your favorite sports team.